I0143206

Little Buddha

A Journey Into Buddhism for Kids

Psalm Carnoustie

Tukotuku Publishing

Book Cover by Tukotuku Publishing

Illustrations by Tukotuku Publishing

First edition 2024

Print ISBN: 978-1-991339-27-0

Ebook ISBN:978-1-991339-28-7

To all the curious minds and kind hearts out there—

This book is for you. May you always ask big questions,

discover small joys, and find peace in every little moment.

Remember, the greatest adventures often start

with a single breath and a curious heart.

With love and light, Psalm Carnoustie

Contents

Welcome to Your Little Buddha Adventure!

Hey there, curious explorer! Welcome to Little Buddha – A Journey into Buddhism for Kids. This isn't just any regular book—it's your golden ticket to a world of wisdom, kindness, and some pretty cool ancient stories. Don't worry, you won't need to sit cross-legged for hours or give up cookies (unless you want to). Instead, you're about to dive into a world where peace isn't just a word—it's something you can feel.

So, what's this book all about? Well, we're going to meet a wise prince named Siddhartha, who became the Buddha—kind of like the original superhero of calm vibes. You'll hear about his epic adventures, his big discoveries, and how he unlocked the secrets of happiness under a very wise tree (yes, trees can be wise too!).

But wait—this isn't just about ancient stories. Nope! We're also going to learn how you can bring a little bit of Buddha magic into your daily life. Ever wonder how breathing could be your superpower? Or how being kind could make you feel like you just discovered a treasure chest? You'll find out!

This book is filled with funny stories, silly examples, and even a few snack breaks (because learning is hard work, right?). Whether you're here to find out what meditation is, why karma isn't just for cats, or how a single thought can change your day, you've come to the right place.

So, grab your favorite reading spot, maybe a snack or two, and let's start this adventure together. By the end, you might just discover that being a 'Little Buddha' isn't about being perfect—it's about being you, but with a little extra kindness, calmness, and curiosity sprinkled on top.

Ready? Take a deep breath, smile, and let's begin!

What in the World is Buddhism?

A Quick Look at Buddha

Imagine a long time ago, in a place called India, there lived a prince named Siddhartha. Now, Siddhartha was not your average prince who spent all day eating cake and playing with toys.

No, he was a curious little guy who wondered why everyone was so grumpy all the time. He had everything a kid could dream of—palaces, toys, and even a pet elephant! But something was missing. So, one day, he decided to sneak out of the palace (with a little help from his magic carpet, ahem, just kidding) to see what was really going on outside those fancy walls.

When Siddhartha stepped out, he saw some pretty surprising things. There were old people, sick people, and people looking really sad. It was like a sad parade! Siddhartha thought, "Yikes! What's going on here?" He realized that life was not just about playing with elephants and eating sweets; it also had its tough moments. Instead of going back to his cozy palace and pretending everything was fine, he decided to find out how to help everyone feel happier. Talk about bravery!

So, Siddhartha took off on a grand adventure. He tried all sorts of things to discover the secret to happiness. He met some wise teachers, experimented with meditation (which is a fancy word for sitting quietly and thinking about nothing, like trying not to think about chocolate cake), and even tried to eat just one grain of rice a day! Can you imagine that? A prince who was hungry all the time! But he was determined to learn. Eventually, after a lot of thinking, he realized that true happiness comes from understanding ourselves and the world around us.

Then one day, while sitting under a big, beautiful tree (called the Bodhi tree, which is basically a tree with a PhD in wisdom), Siddhartha had a light bulb moment. He became the Buddha, which means "the Awakened One." He figured out that life is all about balance, kindness, and understanding. Instead of chasing after sweets and toys, he showed everyone how to find joy by being nice, sharing, and appreciating what you have. He even had a special recipe for happiness, and it didn't include any broccoli!

Soon, people started gathering around Buddha, eager to learn his secrets. He shared stories, laughter, and even some funny parables that taught important lessons. Kids just like you began to realize they could practice kindness, help others, and even find peace in their busy lives. So, the next time you feel a little grumpy or confused, remember Siddhartha's journey. You don't need a magic carpet, just a kind heart and a curious mind to start your own adventure into the wonderful world of Buddhism!

The Four Noble Truths

Not as Scary as They Sound

Imagine you're on a treasure hunt, and you stumble upon a map that looks a little confusing. But guess what? The treasure map is actually the Four Noble Truths! These truths are like a fun guide to understanding life, and they aren't as scary as they might seem. Think of them as four silly but wise friends who want to help you out. So, let's dive into this treasure hunt and discover what these truths are all about!

The first truth is about recognizing that sometimes, life can feel a bit like stepping on a Lego in the dark. It can be painful and confusing! This truth tells us that everyone experiences suffering, whether it's from stubbed toes, losing a favorite toy, or feeling grumpy when things don't go our way. But don't worry! It's just a part of being human, and even the happiest people sometimes get a little sad. It's like realizing that even ice cream can melt!

Now, the second truth is about finding out why we sometimes feel this way. Imagine if a sneaky monster named Craving is hiding under your bed, always asking for more ice cream or more video game time. This truth explains that our desires can sometimes make us feel unhappy. When we want things we can't have, just like Craving under the bed, we can feel frustrated. But here's the good news: understanding this can help us manage our cravings and find happiness in what we already have, like a cozy blanket or a good book!

The third truth is like a magic key that helps us unlock the door to happiness. It tells us that if we let go of our cravings and learn to be content, we can find a way to feel peaceful. It's like learning to enjoy the sunshine instead of worrying about the rain. When we focus on things that make us happy and grateful, we discover that happiness is already inside us! So, instead of searching for happiness in the bottom of an ice cream bowl, we can find it in our hearts and friendships.

Finally, the fourth truth is the treasure map itself! It shows us the path to happiness and peace through the Eightfold Path. This path is like a fun obstacle course where we can practice being kind, making good choices, and paying attention to our thoughts. Each part of the path helps us grow and learn, just like when we practice our favorite hobbies. So, we don't have to take giant leaps; we can take small, happy steps every day!

So, there you have it! The Four Noble Truths are like a playful adventure that can help us understand ourselves better and find joy in our lives. They remind us that it's okay to feel sad sometimes and that we can always find ways to be happier. Embracing these truths is like having a trusty map and a cool guide on our journey through life. Now, let's get out there, explore, and enjoy this incredible adventure together!

Karma

It's Not Just for Cats!

Karma is like a cosmic boomerang; whatever you throw out into the world comes back to you, sometimes with a funny twist! Imagine you're playing catch with your friend and you throw the ball really hard. If you're not careful, you might end up with the ball flying right back at you! In the world of karma, every action you take is like that ball. If you're kind and helpful, you're likely to get kindness and help back. But if you're a bit mischievous, like sneaking cookies from the jar, you might find yourself in a sticky situation!

Now, let's talk about why karma isn't just for cats, even though they seem to know a thing or two about it. Have you ever noticed how your pet cat always seems to land on its feet? That's karma in action! When cats knock something over, they often get a little surprise when their human finds out. But here's the funny part:

while cats might think they're sneaky, they can't escape the karma of their clumsiness. Just like cats, we humans also create our own little whirlwinds of karma with our actions, whether we're being helpful or pulling pranks on our siblings.

Imagine if every time you helped someone, you got a little sticker on a chart. Those stickers are like karma points! The more stickers you collect, the more awesome things might happen to you. Maybe your friend will share their favorite snack, or your teacher will give you a high-five for being helpful in class. On the flip side, if you spend your time being a couch potato who never helps out, you might find that no one wants to share their toys with you. Just like in a video game, the choices you make can lead to different outcomes, and karma is the magical scorekeeper!

Karma is also pretty sneaky when it comes to emotions. Let's say you're having a rough day and decide to take it out on your friends by being grumpy. That's like throwing a water balloon at them, but instead of water, it's filled with frowns and grumbles.

Guess what? That frown might come back to you when your friends decide to play without you! But if you choose to spread smiles and laughter, you might just find yourself surrounded by happy pals who want to share their games with you. It's all about the energy you put out into the world!

So, remember, karma is like a silly dance! When you do the right moves—like being kind, helpful, and cheerful—you'll find that life dances back with you, bringing joy and good vibes. But if you decide to do the funky chicken of mischief, don't be surprised if you trip over your own feet! As you start your journey into Buddhism, think of karma as your friendly guide, encouraging you to make choices that not only make you happy but also sprinkle a little happiness around you, just like a disco ball lighting up a party!

Fun Stories from the Buddha's Life

The Time Buddha Got a Haircut

O nce upon a time, in a land far, far away, there was a young prince named Siddhartha. He lived in a giant palace filled with treasures, delicious food, and, of course, lots of fluffy pillows. But one day, Siddhartha looked in the mirror and thought, "Wow, my hair is getting out of control!" It was long, tangled, and looked like a bird might have made a nest in it. He decided it was time for a haircut, and little did he know, this simple act would change his life forever!

Siddhartha marched his way to the royal barber, who was known for giving the best haircuts in the kingdom. As the barber began to snip away at Siddhartha's long locks, the prince couldn't help but giggle. "Is it just me, or does my hair look like spaghetti?" he joked.

The barber laughed so hard he almost dropped his scissors! But as his hair fell to the ground, Siddhartha started to feel a strange tickle in his heart. "Why do I have all this fancy stuff when outside the palace, people are suffering?" he wondered.

After his haircut, Siddhartha decided to sneak out of the palace to see the world beyond the walls. He put on a simple robe and left his fancy shoes behind. As he walked through the village, he spotted a child crying over a broken toy, an old man who looked tired and sad, and a woman who was struggling to carry heavy baskets. Siddhartha realized that life wasn't all about pretty hair or fancy clothes; it was about helping others and finding happiness. "I have to do something!" he exclaimed, making his hairless head shine brighter than ever.

Determined to make a difference, Siddhartha decided to give up his princely life. He told his family he was going on a special adventure. "Mom, Dad, I'm off to find the secret to happiness!" And with that, he waved goodbye, leaving behind his fancy palace and all his treasures. Instead, he wore a simple robe and started to live like the people he had seen in the village. Siddhartha realized that sometimes, when you let go of the things you think you need, like his long, fancy hair, you can discover something much more important: a happy heart!

As he wandered from place to place, Siddhartha met many interesting people and learned from them. He practiced kindness, meditation, and even found joy in nature, like watching the clouds float by and listening to the birds sing. And guess what? That haircut wasn't just about looking different; it was the first step on Siddhartha's journey to becoming the Buddha, the Enlightened One! So the next time you need a haircut or a change, remember Siddhartha and how a little snip could lead to discovering the best version of yourself!

The Elephant Who Thought He Was a Mouse

O nce upon a time in a lush, green jungle, there lived an elephant named Ellie. Now, Ellie was no ordinary elephant. While most elephants stomped around with confidence, Ellie had a peculiar belief: she thought she was a mouse! Every morning, she would look at her reflection in the water and say, "Oh, what a tiny and adorable mouse I am!" The other animals would giggle, but Ellie was determined to live her best mouse life, complete with squeaky sounds and attempts to hide in the smallest bushes.

Ellie loved to munch on acorns and nibble on cheese crumbs, which was quite the challenge for someone with her big trunk and enormous feet! One day, while attempting to squeeze into a mouse-sized hole in a tree, Ellie got stuck! The other animals gathered around, laughing and cheering. "Come on, Ellie! You can do it!" they shouted. But no matter how hard she tried, her big, fluffy body just wouldn't fit. It turned into a hilarious jungle spectacle, and even the wise old owl couldn't help but chuckle. "Maybe it's time to accept you're an elephant, my friend!" he hooted.

Feeling a bit embarrassed but still determined, Ellie decided to seek advice from her friend, Benny the wise tortoise. "Benny, how can I be the best mouse ever?" she asked earnestly. Benny smiled slowly and replied, "Dear Ellie, you are wonderful just the way you are! You don't need to be small to be special. Being an elephant means you can help others and be strong!" Ellie thought about this for a moment. "You mean I can be a big, fabulous elephant and still be special?" she asked, her ears flapping with excitement.

The very next day, Ellie woke up with a new mindset. Instead of trying to be a mouse, she decided to use her size to help her friends. She could reach the highest fruits for the birds and create shade for the smaller animals during the hot days. Ellie even started a "Big and Bold Club" where all her friends could join and celebrate their unique qualities, whether they were big, small, furry, or feathered. Everyone had a blast, and Ellie learned that being herself was the best thing she could be!

By embracing her true self, Ellie discovered the joy of being an elephant while also sharing her love with others. It taught her an important lesson about self-acceptance, a little like what the Buddha teaches us about being true to ourselves. Just like Ellie, you don't have to be like anyone else to be special. So, whether you're a big elephant or a tiny mouse, remember that everyone has their own unique role in the world, and that's what makes life so wonderfully funny and interesting!

Buddha and the Hungry Ghosts

O nce upon a time in a land filled with green hills and blossoming flowers, Buddha was taking a nice leisurely stroll. He loved to walk and think, but this time he stumbled upon a group of hungry ghosts. These were not your regular ghosts that pop up during Halloween; they were special! They had enormous bellies but tiny mouths, which meant they were always hungry and never satisfied. Imagine trying to eat spaghetti with a teeny-tiny fork! The ghosts were so grumpy that even the butterflies were scared to flutter by.

Buddha, being the wise and friendly teacher he was, decided to help these hungry ghosts. He noticed them looking longingly at delicious food but unable to eat it. "Why don't you just have a snack?" he asked, scratching his head. The ghosts replied, "We can't! Our mouths are so small that we can only nibble at crumbs!" Buddha thought for a moment and then came up with a brilliant idea. "What if we all share a big meal together?" he suggested, his eyes twinkling like stars.

Buddha gathered all the villagers and explained his plan. Everyone was excited! They cooked up a feast that would make even the grumpiest ghost smile. There were golden rice, juicy fruits, and even sweet cakes! As the villagers set the table, Buddha reminded everyone, "Sharing is the best way to fill our hearts and bellies!"

The hungry ghosts watched with their eyes wide open, and even their tiny mouths began to water. It was the most magical moment—their bellies rumbled like thunder!

When the feast began, Buddha encouraged everyone to serve the ghosts first. As the villagers filled the ghosts' plates, something incredible happened! The ghosts discovered that when they shared food with others, their tiny mouths became bigger! They could take big bites and enjoy every morsel. They laughed and giggled as they devoured the food, and soon their grumpy faces turned into happy smiles. Buddha was delighted; he knew that sharing not only filled bellies but also made hearts glow with joy.

From that day on, the hungry ghosts learned a valuable lesson: being kind and sharing with others can change everything! They promised to help Buddha spread joy and kindness wherever they floated. And so, whenever they heard someone say, "I'm hungry," they would swoosh in with a feast, reminding everyone that sharing and caring make the world a happier place. So, if you ever feel a little grumpy or hungry, just re-member Buddha and the hungry ghosts. Maybe you can share a snack with a friend and fill not just your belly, but your heart too!

Silly Folktales with a Twist

The Tortoise and the Buddha

Once upon a time in a peaceful forest, there lived a tortoise named Tilly. Tilly wasn't just any tortoise; she had a knack for thinking deep thoughts. One sunny afternoon, while munching on some delicious leaves, Tilly decided that she wanted to learn more about life, happiness, and, of course, the wise Buddha! So, with a determined look on her face, she set off on a little adventure to find him. But first, she had to figure out how to move a little faster than her usual "tortoise pace."

As Tilly waddled along, she met Benny the Bunny, who was bouncing around like he had a spring in his step. "Hey there, Tilly! Where are you off to?" Benny asked, twitching his ears. "I'm on a quest to learn about the Buddha!" Tilly exclaimed. Benny giggled, "You're a tortoise on a quest? That sounds like a slow-motion movie!" Tilly chuckled back, "Well, every great adventure starts with a little bit of slow!" And off they went, hopping and waddling down the path, discussing how the Buddha taught kindness, peace, and how to be happy.

After what felt like an eternity (for a tortoise, anyway), Tilly and Benny finally stumbled upon a serene meadow where the Buddha was sitting under a big, shady tree. Tilly was so excited that she nearly did a somersault! The Buddha smiled warmly and said, "Hello, my friends! What brings you to my little corner of the world?" Tilly took a deep breath and replied, "I want to know how to be happy and wise like you!" The Buddha chuckled softly, "Well, my dear tortoise, happiness comes from understanding yourself and being kind to others."

As the day went on, Tilly learned that it's not about how fast you run or hop, but about the journey you take and the friends you make along the way. The Buddha shared stories about how even small acts of kindness can create ripples of happiness, just like throwing a pebble into a pond.

Tilly realized that being a tortoise had its perks. She could take her time, enjoy the beauty of the flowers, and appreciate every little thing around her while learning to be mindful, just like the Buddha taught.

When it was time to say goodbye, Tilly felt a warm glow in her heart. She thanked the Buddha and hopped back into the forest with Benny by her side. "You know, Tilly," Benny said, "you might be slow, but you're one of the wisest tortoises I know!" Tilly smiled, her shell shining in the sun. "And I'm the happiest tortoise, thanks to the Buddha!" From that day on, Tilly shared her newfound wisdom with all her forest friends, proving that even a little tortoise can lead a great adventure when it comes to understanding kindness, happiness, and the teachings of the Buddha.

The Monkey Who Learned to Meditate

O nce upon a time in a lush green jungle, there lived a cheeky little monkey named Momo. Momo was not your average monkey; he loved swinging from trees and munching on bananas, but he also had a big problem. He could never sit still!

While all the other animals were busy meditating, Momo was busy bouncing around, doing flips, and making funny faces. His friends often said, "Momo, if you could just sit quietly for one minute, you might discover the secrets of the jungle!" But who wants to sit still when there are so many fun things to do?

One sunny day, Momo spotted a wise old tortoise named Tashi who was known for his incredible ability to meditate. Tashi sat by the riverbank, looking as calm as a pond on a still day. Momo thought this was the perfect chance to learn something new. So, he scampered over and asked, "Tashi, can you teach me how to meditate? I want to be as cool as you!" Tashi chuckled softly, "Of course, little monkey! But first, you must learn to be still and quiet. Can you do that?" Momo scratched his head and said, "I can try... but it might be a bouncy challenge!"

The next day, Momo decided to give meditation a shot. He found a cozy spot on a thick branch and took a deep breath. "Okay, Momo, just sit still," he told himself. But as soon as he closed his eyes, he felt a tickle on his nose! It was a butterfly, flapping its wings. Momo swatted at it, lost his balance, and tumbled off the branch. "Well, that didn't go as planned!" he laughed, shaking off the leaves. Tashi watched from afar, shaking his head with a gentle smile. "Remember, Momo, meditation is about being present, even when things get a little silly."

Determined to improve, Momo returned to Tashi every day for advice. Tashi taught him to focus on his breath and to let thoughts float away like leaves on the river. "Just imagine each thought is a banana," Tashi said. "You can look at it, but don't grab it!" Momo giggled at the idea of bananas floating by, and soon he found himself sitting a little longer without bouncing around. "This is kind of fun!" he squeaked, "but I still can't resist a good somersault now and then!"

After a few weeks of practice, Momo discovered that he could meditate, even if it meant having a few giggles along the way. He learned to appreciate the quiet moments and found that meditation made him feel happy and calm, like a gentle breeze in the jungle. One day, as he sat quietly, he noticed the beautiful flowers, the rustling leaves, and even the sound of a distant waterfall. "Wow, I can see the jungle in a whole new way!" Momo exclaimed. From that day on, Momo became the coolest little monkey in the jungle, showing everyone that meditation could be a fun adventure, even for the bounciest of creatures!

The Wise Old Owl and the Curious Rabbit

Once upon a time, in a lush green forest filled with chirping birds and buzzing bees, lived a wise old owl named Ollie. Ollie was known far and wide for his incredible knowledge and his love of napping. He spent his days perched high up in a sturdy oak tree, dozing off while keeping one eye open just in case someone needed his advice. One sunny afternoon, a curious little rabbit named Ruby hopped by, her nose twitching with excitement. "Ollie! Ollie! Wake up! I have so many questions!" she squeaked, her fluffy tail bouncing behind her.

Ollie opened one eye and let out a sleepy hoot. "Questions, you say? Well, I'm not a question-answering machine like those fancy robots! But go on, I'm all ears... sort of," he chuckled, trying to shake off his drowsiness. Ruby, undeterred by his sleepy demeanor, began firing questions like a mini-firecracker. "Why do we have to be kind? What's the meaning of life? How do you stay so wise?" Ollie listened carefully, each question making him feel more awake. "Ah, the meaning of life! That's a big one, my dear rabbit. It's not about hopping around or munching on carrots," he said, winking at her.

With a twinkle in his eye, Ollie decided to share a little secret. "The secret is mindfulness! It means paying attention to what you're doing and being present. If you're munching on a carrot, really enjoy that carrot! Imagine it's the best carrot in the world!" Ruby's ears perked up. "So, if I pay attention to my carrot, it'll be tastier?" she asked, her mouth watering at the thought. "Exactly!" Ollie hooted, "And it will help you appreciate everything around you, like the beautiful flowers and the gentle breeze. Mindfulness is a superpower every kid can have!"

Feeling inspired, Ruby jumped up and down. "Ollie, what other superpowers can we learn?" Ollie chuckled again, this time a bit louder. "Well, there's compassion! That means being kind and understanding to others, just like how you share your carrots with your friends. And then there's patience, which is like waiting for your favorite vegetable to grow. It can be hard, but it's worth it!" Ruby nodded vigorously, imagining all the delicious veggies she could share, and the excitement of waiting for them to grow. "So, being wise is all about practicing these things?" she asked, her eyes shining with curiosity.

"Absolutely, my fluffy friend! And remember, even wise owls take naps," Ollie said with a playful wink. Ruby giggled, "I'll practice mindfulness while I nap too!" As the sun began to set, painting the sky in shades of orange and pink, Ruby hopped away with a head full of ideas and a heart brimming with joy. Ollie settled back onto his branch, closing his eyes with a smile, knowing he had shared a bit of wisdom with a curious little rabbit. After all, the journey into understanding Buddhism was just beginning, and every question, every moment of mindfulness, was a step along the way.

Simple Practices for Little Buddhas

Breathing Like a Pro (and a Buddah)

B reathing is something we all do, like sneezing or eating

ice cream, but did you know that there's a way to breathe like a pro? Imagine being able to take a deep breath and feel as calm as a turtle lounging on a sunny rock. In Buddhism, breathing is super important! It can help us feel relaxed, focused, and ready to tackle any challenge—like a math test or a surprise broccoli dinner. So let's dive into the world of breathing like a true Buddha!

Now, what does it mean to breathe like a Buddha? First, we have to find our special "breathing spot." It could be your bedroom, a cozy corner of the living room, or even under your favorite tree in the backyard. Once you find your spot, sit down comfortably. You can cross your legs like a pretzel or sit on a chair like a wise old owl. The key here is to get comfy and let your body relax like a floppy pancake. Ready? Let's get to work on our breathing!

Here's the fun part! Take a big breath in through your nose—like you're sniffing a delicious slice of pizza. Hold it for a moment, and then whoosh it out through your mouth like you're blowing out birthday candles. Do this a few times, and you'll feel as if you're floating on a fluffy cloud. Remember, if you accidentally make funny noises while breathing, that's totally okay! Even Buddhas giggle sometimes, especially when they're trying not to laugh at their own funny faces.

Now that we're pros at breathing, let's add a splash of imagination. Picture your breath as a magical wave rolling in and out, bringing calmness and happiness. With every breath in, imagine you're filling up with bright, happy sunshine, and with every breath out, let go of any worries—like tossing away a stinky sock. This fun little trick can help us feel better when we're sad, angry, or just having a "meh" day. Who knew breathing could be such a superhero?

Finally, let's remember that breathing isn't just for the quiet moments. You can use it anytime—before a big game, during a boring car ride, or even when your little brother is being extra annoying. Just take a deep breath, and you'll feel like you have a superpower! So, practice your pro-breathing skills every day, and soon you'll be the coolest little Buddha around, spreading calmness, joy, and maybe even a few giggles wherever you go!

Mindfulness

Being Present Without the Presents

Being present means paying attention to what's happening right now, and it's a bit like trying to catch a butterfly with your bare hands. You see, when you're busy thinking about what happened yesterday or what might happen tomorrow, you're more like a butterfly that's already flown away. Mindfulness is all about gently bringing your focus back to the here and now, like a friendly little squirrel reminding you to stop chasing after acorns from last week!

Imagine you're at a birthday party, and everyone is munching on cake. Instead of worrying about how many slices you can eat or what games you'll play later, you can take a deep breath and really enjoy that first bite of cake. Is it chocolate? Vanilla? Strawberry? Mindfulness lets you savor the flavors, like a detective solving the delicious mystery of what's in your mouth! It's like being a cake detective on an important mission, but instead of finding a missing cake, you find joy in every crumb!

Sometimes, our minds are like a busy bee buzzing around, flitting from thought to thought. "What's for dinner? Did I forget my homework? Ooh, look at that squirrel!" Mindfulness helps us calm that bee down. We can sit quietly, focus on our breathing, and let the busy thoughts float away like clouds in the sky. When we do this, it's like opening a window in a stuffy room and letting fresh air in. Suddenly, everything feels clearer, and we can really see the world around us—like the bright colors of the leaves or the silly faces our friends make when they laugh!

Now, let's imagine you're outside, lying on the grass, and you spot a fluffy cloud shaped like a dinosaur. Instead of jumping up to tell everyone, you take a moment to just enjoy that sight. You can think, "Wow, that cloud is huge! I wonder if I'll ever see a real dinosaur." This is mindfulness at work. It's about being fully engaged in the moment, whether you're looking at clouds, playing with friends, or even just feeling the sunshine on your face. It helps us appreciate the little things, like the smell of flowers or the sound of laughter.

So, how can you practice mindfulness in your daily life? Start small! Try taking a minute each day to close your eyes, breathe deeply, and listen to the sounds around you. Is that the rustling of leaves? The chirping of birds? Or maybe it's your pet snoring like a little monster? Remember, being present doesn't need fancy gifts or presents; it just takes a curious heart and a little bit of practice. So next time you feel your mind racing like a car on a racetrack, just slow down, take a deep breath, and enjoy the ride!

The Life of the Buddha

A Kid-Friendly Biography

Born in a Palace, But Not a Spoiled Kid

Once upon a time, in a grand palace filled with sparkling jewels and fluffy pillows, a baby named Siddhartha was born. The king and queen were so excited that they threw a huge party with dancing elephants and a cake the size of a small mountain. But here's the funny part: even though Siddhartha was born in a palace, he wasn't just a spoiled little prince who ate sweets all day. Nope! He was as curious as a cat and loved to explore the world around him, even if that meant getting his royal clothes a bit dusty.

While other kids in the palace were busy playing with their shiny toys, Siddhartha had a different idea of fun. He would sneak out into the garden, where he met all sorts of creatures. One day, he spotted a tiny ant trying to climb over a big rock. Instead of laughing at the ant's struggle, Siddhartha decided to help. He carefully picked up the rock and placed it aside, all while imagining what it would be like to be an ant. "I bet they have the best adventures!" he thought. This showed that even though he lived in luxury, he cared about the little things and the little creatures.

Siddhartha loved nature more than anything. He would chase butterflies, play with flowers, and even talk to the trees. The other kids might have been inside, playing with their fancy toys, but Siddhartha was out there making friends with the squirrels. One time, he even asked a wise old turtle for advice on life. The turtle, moving at its own slow pace, said, "Patience, young prince! Life is more than just a race!" Siddhartha chuckled and realized that even royalty needed to slow down sometimes.

But here's the best part: Siddhartha never thought he was better than anyone else just because he was a prince. He saw everyone as equal, whether they were rich or poor, big or small. He would often share his toys and snacks with the other kids in the village. When they played together, he would say, "Let's build the biggest sandcastle ever!" and they would laugh as they worked together, forgetting about their differences. Siddhartha knew that kindness was not about where you came from, but how you treat others.

As years went by, Siddhartha learned valuable lessons about happiness, friendship, and caring for others. He understood that true joy didn't come from having a palace full of toys but from making connections with people and nature. So, the next time you feel a bit spoiled or want to keep everything for yourself, think of Siddhartha and his adventures. Remember that sharing, caring, and exploring the world around you can lead to the greatest treasures of all—friendship and happiness!

The Great Escape

Buddha's Adventure Out of the Palace

Once upon a time, in a land filled with the sounds of laughter and the smell of delicious food, there lived a young prince named Siddhartha. Siddhartha was no ordinary kid; he lived in a grand palace with shiny chandeliers and delicious meals served on golden plates. You might think, "Wow, what a lucky kid!" But Siddhartha was not so sure. In fact, he was a bit bored. You see, his father wanted to protect him from the outside world, so he never let him leave the palace. So Siddhartha decided it was time for a little adventure.

One sunny day, Siddhartha woke up with a spark in his eyes. He couldn't take it anymore! He wanted to see what was beyond the palace walls. So, he put on his sneakiest outfit—well, it was just his regular clothes, but he imagined he looked like a ninja. He tiptoed past his sleeping guards, who were probably dreaming of giant cupcakes, and out the big palace doors. "I'm free!" he shouted, though he quickly covered his mouth, worried someone might hear him.

As Siddhartha stepped outside, he was amazed. The vibrant colors of the flowers danced in the sunlight, and the laughter of children filled the air. He saw a little boy playing with his puppy, and a group of girls giggling as they skipped rope. "What is this magical place?" he wondered. It was so much more fun than the palace, where he had to practice his princely duties like bowing and eating with a fancy fork. Siddhartha felt like he had just discovered a treasure chest filled with joy!

But then, he noticed something strange. As he explored further, he saw an old man with a cane, a sick person lying in a bed, and a sad woman crying by the river. Siddhartha's heart sank. "What's going on?" he thought. "Why does everyone not look like they're having fun?" For the first time, he realized that life was not just about laughter and shiny things. There were challenges, too, and that made him think deeply. Siddhartha felt like a superhero who needed to understand how to help people, not just have fun.

After a long day of adventures, Siddhartha returned to the palace, but he was different now. He had discovered the wonders and challenges of the world outside and wanted to learn more about them. He realized that being a prince was not just about living in luxury; it was about understanding and caring for others. So, with a heart full of curiosity and determination, he began his journey to find answers. Who knew that a simple trip outside the palace could lead to such a great adventure? Siddhartha's journey was just beginning, and he was ready to explore the mysteries of life, one little step at a time!

Finding Enlightenment

A Journey with Snacks

Have you ever thought about how snacks can lead to enlightenment? Well, grab your favorite treat, because we're about to munch our way through a delicious adventure! Picture this: you're sitting under a tree, just like the famous Buddha did, with a bag of crunchy snacks. As you take a bite, you realize that every snack can teach you something about life and help you on your journey to being a little Buddha yourself!

First, let's talk about popcorn. Imagine that every kernel is like a thought bouncing around in your head. When you pop a kernel, it bursts into a fluffy piece of goodness! Sometimes, we need to let our thoughts pop and expand, just like that popcorn. When you're worried or sad, take a moment to enjoy some popcorn and let those thoughts pop away.

Who knew that a movie snack could help us practice mindfulness and let our worries float away like the popcorn in the air?

Now, let's munch on some chocolate. Chocolate can be a little like the sweetness of kindness. When you share a piece with a friend, it's like spreading joy all around! Buddha taught us that kindness is important, and sharing snacks is a fun way to practice it. So next time you're enjoying a chocolate bar, think about how sharing it can make both you and your friend feel warm and fuzzy inside, just like the chocolate melting in your mouth!

Don't forget about fruits! Apples, bananas, and oranges are nature's candy, and they remind us of the beauty of the world around us. When you take a bite of a juicy apple, think about how it grew from a tiny seed into something delicious. This is a little like how we all grow and learn. Every time you enjoy a fruit, you're also appreciating nature and the hard work that goes into making it. So, while you're munching, remember to be grateful for the earth, just like the Buddha appreciated everything around him.

Finally, let's not skip dessert! Cookies can represent balance in our lives. Sometimes it's okay to indulge, but just like too many cookies can give you a tummy ache, too much of anything can throw you off balance. Buddha taught us to find the middle way, which means enjoying life without overdoing it. So, the next time you're dunking a cookie in milk, think about how you can enjoy treats while still keeping your body and mind happy and healthy. Finding enlightenment can be a tasty journey full of snacks, laughter, and important lessons!

Nature and Buddhism

Finding Buddha in the Great Outdoors

Buddha and the Beautiful Trees

O nce upon a time, in a land filled with sunshine and friendly animals, there lived a very wise man named Buddha.

You might think Buddha was just a regular guy, but he was special because he had a big heart and an even bigger mind. One sunny afternoon, Buddha decided to take a stroll through the forest. The trees were laughing with the wind, and the flowers were having a dance party! Buddha loved nature, and guess what? The trees loved Buddha right back! They would sway and rustle their leaves, almost like they were waving hello.

As Buddha walked, he came across a tree that was taller than a giraffe wearing platform shoes. It was so tall that Buddha thought it might have its own cloud! "Hello, Tall Tree!" Buddha said with a grin. "What's it like being so high up?" The tree chuckled and replied, "Oh, Buddha, up here the view is fantastic! I can see the whole forest, and sometimes I even get a peek at the fluffy clouds playing tag!" Buddha laughed and thought how wonderful it would be to see the world from up high, but then the tree added, "But you know, being down here isn't so bad either. I get to watch all the little animals and kids like you having fun!"

As he continued his walk, Buddha found a small tree that looked a bit sad. Its leaves were drooping, and it seemed to be frowning. "Why the long face, Little Tree?" Buddha asked, kneeling down to listen closely. The Little Tree sighed, "I feel so small and unimportant compared to the Tall Tree. I wish I could grow big and strong!" Buddha smiled and said, "Oh, Little Tree, being small has its own superpowers! You can wiggle in the breeze, give shade to tiny critters, and grow delicious fruits for kids to munch on. Plus, you're close to the ground where all the fun is happening!"

Buddha decided to teach the Little Tree about the magic of being yourself. "You see, every tree has a special job. The Tall Tree shares its view, and you share your sweetness! Just like how everyone in the world is different, we all have our own talents. It's not about being the biggest; it's about being the best version of YOU!" The Little Tree perked up, feeling a little taller already. It realized that being small was pretty cool after all, especially when you could help a squirrel find a snack!

As the sun began to set, casting a golden glow over the forest, Buddha waved goodbye to his leafy friends. He felt grateful for the beautiful trees that taught him so much about life. Each tree, whether tall or small, had its own story and wisdom to share. Buddha decided then and there that every day, he would remind kids like you to appreciate the beauty around you and the unique gifts you have. So, the next time you see a tree, remember Buddha's lesson, give it a smile, and think about how special you are, just like that Little Tree!

Animals

Buddha's Furry Friends

Once upon a time in ancient India, there was a little prince named Siddhartha, who later became known as Buddha. But did you know that Siddhartha had some furry friends? That's right! Animals were not just his buddies; they were also his teachers. Imagine a prince sitting under a tree, surrounded by a bunch

of curious monkeys, wise elephants, and even a few chatty
birds! These animals were always
up to something funny, making Siddhartha giggle and sometimes even teaching him important lessons about life.

One day, Siddhartha was wander-
ing in the forest when he stumbled upon a mischievous monkey
swinging from branch to branch.
The monkey was so good at climbing that it made Siddhartha think,
"Wow! If only I could jump around
like that!" But then he remem-
bered something very important:
it's not about jumping high; it's

about being kind and gentle, just like the monkey shared his bananas with his friends. So Siddhartha decided that sharing was way more fun than being the best climber in the forest. Plus, who wouldn't want to share bananas?

Then there was a wise old elephant who would often stop by to visit Siddhartha. This elephant had a big ear for listening and a bigger heart for caring. One day, the elephant told Siddhartha, "You know, being strong is great, but being gentle is even better." Siddhartha thought about that while petting the elephant's trunk, which was surprisingly soft. It reminded him that sometimes, the biggest strength comes from being kind and understanding, just like the elephant who shared his wisdom without any fuss.

Siddhartha's furry friends also helped him understand the importance of being present. One sunny afternoon, he watched a group of squirrels scurrying around, gathering nuts. They were so busy and focused that it made him laugh! It was like they were in a tiny squirrel race. He learned that just like those squirrels, he needed to pay attention to what was happening around him and appreciate the little things in life, like the sound of rustling leaves or the smell of blooming flowers.

As Siddhartha grew wiser, he realized that animals could teach us about love, compassion, and being in the moment. He understood that even the smallest creature had something valuable to share. So next time you see a furry friend, whether it's a cat, dog, or even a friendly squirrel, remember that they might have a lesson for you. Maybe they'll remind you to be silly, share your snacks, listen carefully, or just enjoy the sunshine. After all, every animal has a story, and sometimes, the best friends are the ones with fur!

Nature Walks

Adventures with Mindfulness

Nature walks are like a treasure hunt, but instead of searching for gold coins or sparkling jewels, you're on the lookout for amazing plants, funny animals, and maybe even a ninja squirrel! Imagine putting on your explorer hat, grabbing a magnifying glass, and heading out into the great outdoors. Each step you take is a new adventure, filled with the sounds of chirping birds and the rustle of leaves. Who knows, you might even find a stick that looks just like a dragon!

As you stroll through the park or your backyard, take a moment to notice everything around you. Did you see that butterfly flapping its wings like it's practicing for a dance-off? Or the way the wind tickles the grass, making it sway like it's doing a happy jig? Mindfulness is all about being aware of what's happening right now, and nature is the perfect place to practice. So, give your brain a break from thinking about lunch or that video game, and focus on the wonders of the world around you!

Maybe you've heard about the wise old owl that knows all the secrets of the forest. Well, if you listen closely during your nature walk, you might just hear some of those secrets! The trees have stories to tell, the flowers are gossiping about the bees, and the rocks are keeping the biggest secrets. Every little thing in nature has its own story, just like you do! Imagine if you could tell the story of the fluffy cloud that looks like a unicorn. You could call it "The Adventures of Sir Fluffington the Cloud!"

If you ever feel a bit grumpy or bored during your nature walk, just remember that it's completely normal. Sometimes, a little stroll can turn into a comedy show! You might trip over a root and do an unintentional dance move or get chased by a curious squirrel who thinks you have snacks. These moments are like little giggles from the universe, reminding you not to take life too seriously. Laughing at yourself is a great way to practice being mindful and enjoying the present!

At the end of your nature walk, take a moment to sit down, close your eyes, and breathe in the fresh air. Think about all the funny things you saw and the silly moments you had. Just like the Buddha taught us about being in the moment, nature walks can help you connect with yourself and the world around you. So, tie your shoelaces, grab your walking stick (or a cool stick you found), and head out for an adventure! Who knows what amazing, funny, and delightful things you'll discover on your journey?

Feeling Good

Buddhism and Emotional Well-being

Understanding Emotions: The Roller Coaster Ride

Imagine your feelings as a roller coaster ride. One minute you're climbing up the tracks, feeling excited and happy, and the next, you're zooming down, feeling scared or a little grumpy. It's a wild adventure that can make your tummy feel funny! Just like the twists and turns of a roller coaster, our emotions can change from joy to sadness, from anger to calmness, all in the blink of an eye. So, buckle up, because understanding our feelings is a fun way to ride through life!

Sometimes, when you wake up in the morning, you might feel like a superhero ready to save the day, wearing your cape and all. But then, out of nowhere, someone accidentally spills juice on your favorite shirt, and suddenly you feel like a balloon that just lost all its air. That's okay! It happens to everyone, even to the coolest monks. They also have days when they feel like they're stuck on the lowest loop of a roller coaster, but they know that it's just part of the ride. Remember, it's perfectly normal to feel all sorts of things, and each feeling is like a colorful car on your emotional roller coaster.

Now, you might wonder why we ride this roller coaster of emotions in the first place. Well, think of it as your heart having a dance party! Happiness makes everyone do the chicken dance, while sadness might have them sitting quietly in a corner. Each emotion has a special role to play in our lives, just like each ride at an amusement park has its own fun. When we learn to recognize and understand these feelings, we can join the party instead of letting them throw us off the ride.

Buddhism teaches us that it's okay to feel all these emotions. In fact, it encourages us to sit with them, kind of like waiting in line for the best ride at the park. Instead of screaming or crying, we can take a deep breath and say, "Hello, feeling! What do you want to teach me today?" This way, we learn that emotions are not just silly ups and downs; they can be wise teachers showing us how to navigate life's bumpy tracks.

So, the next time you feel like you're on a wild roller coaster of emotions, remember to smile and enjoy the ride. Whether you're feeling happy like a puppy or grumpy like a cat that just had a bath, each emotion is part of your adventure. Embrace them all, and you'll discover that every twist and turn can lead to something wonderful, just like a thrilling amusement park day filled with laughter, surprises, and maybe even a little ice cream!

Kindness The Secret Superpower

The Secret Superpower

Kindness is like a secret superpower that everyone has, even if they don't wear capes or fly around like superheroes. Imagine if you had a magical wand that could make people smile just by waving it! Well, guess what? Kindness works just like that. When you share your toys, help a friend who has fallen, or simply say something nice, you're using your superpower to make the world a better place. And the best part? You don't need to train in a secret dojo; you just have to be you!

Let's think about some funny situations that show how kindness can change everything! Picture this: a grumpy cat named Mr. Whiskers, who has a permanent scowl on his furry face. One day, a little boy named Timmy shares his favorite snack, a crunchy carrot, with Mr. Whiskers. Suddenly, the cat's scowl disappears, and he starts dancing like a rockstar! Okay, maybe not dancing, but he does purr and rub against Timmy. That's the magic of kindness! It can turn even the grumpiest of creatures into your new best friend.

You might be wondering how kindness fits into Buddhism. Well, Buddhism teaches us about compassion, which is like a super-charged version of kindness. It's all about understanding how others feel and wanting to help them. Imagine if everyone in your class decided to be compassionate and started helping each other with homework or sharing snacks. Your classroom would be like a big happy bubble of joy! Plus, when you practice kindness, it can make you feel all warm and fuzzy inside, just like a cozy blanket on a chilly day.

Now, let's make being kind a fun adventure! You can create a "Kindness Challenge" with your family or friends. Each week, pick a new mission, like saying something nice to at least five people or helping someone carry their backpack. You could even write silly poems about kindness and share them during show-and-tell. The more you spread kindness, the more it will bounce back to you like a rubber ball. It's like having your own kindness boomerang!

In the end, remember that your superpower of kindness doesn't need a cape or a special costume. It just needs a big heart and a smile. Whenever you choose to be kind, you're not only making others happy, but you're also join-ing a team of superheroes who make the world a brighter place. So, let's unleash our secret super-

power and see how many smiles
we can create together!

Gratitude

Thank You, Universe!

Gratitude is like your favorite superhero cape; it has the magical power to make everything feel better! Imagine you just finished a big bowl of ice cream, and your tummy is doing a happy dance. That's gratitude! It's the feeling you get when you think about all the cool stuff in your life, like your family, your friends, and even your pet goldfish who does tricks. When we say, "Thank you, Universe!" we're like mini-wizards casting a spell of happiness that chases away the grumpy clouds.

Now, let's take a moment to think about what gratitude looks like in action. Picture this: you're at school, and your friend shares their extra cookies with you. What do you do? You might jump up and down, do a little happy jig, and shout, "Thank you!" This is not just a polite thing to say; it's your way of sending a big, warm hug to the Universe. It's like sending a thank-you note to a magical being who is busy making sure you have cookies, sunshine, and maybe even a cool new video game!

But wait, there's more! Gratitude also helps us feel like super-heroes in our own lives. When we focus on the things we appreciate, it's like wearing special gratitude glasses. Everything looks brighter, like a rainbow after the rain. You might even find yourself thanking your teacher for the fun math game or your little brother for being your best sidekick in a superhero mission. By expressing gratitude, we not only make ourselves feel good but also spread joy like confetti to every-one around us!

Let's not forget the little things, like the sound of birds singing or the smell of popcorn at the movies. These tiny moments can fill our hearts with happiness if we take the time to notice them. Every time you say "thank you" for something, it's like planting a magical seed in the garden of your heart, which grows into a beautiful flower of joy. And guess what? The more gratitude you practice, the more flowers bloom, making your garden of happiness super lush and vibrant!

So, kids, as you embark on your journey into Buddhism, remember to keep your gratitude cape handy. It's your secret weapon against grumpiness and sadness. Whenever you feel a little down or overwhelmed, just look around and think of all the wonderful things in your life. Say, "Thank you, Universe!" and feel the happiness wash over you like a warm, fluffy blanket. With gratitude in your heart, every day can be an adventure filled with joy, laughter, and a sprinkle of magic!

Becoming a Little Buddha

Sharing and Caring: The Little Things Matter

In the bustling world of little things, imagine how sharing a cookie can turn a friend's frown upside down! When you grab that last chocolate chip cookie and offer it to someone, you're not just sharing a treat; you're sharing happiness. It's like sprinkling joy all around, and guess what? That's a little bit like what Buddha taught. So, the next time you have something tasty, whether it's a cookie, a candy, or even a cool sticker, remember how great it feels to share. It can make you feel like a superhero, zapping away sadness!

Now, let's talk about caring. Caring is like giving your favorite toy a cozy blanket and a cup of tea. Just kidding! Toys don't drink tea, but they do appreciate a little love. When you take care of your friends, family, or even your pet goldfish, you're practicing kindness. Buddha believed that kindness is a superpower! So, if your friend is having a tough day, a friendly note or a silly drawing can brighten their mood like a rainbow after a rainy day. Little acts of caring can create big waves of happiness.

Have you ever noticed how tiny things can bring giggles? Like when you see a squirrel doing a funny dance or a dog chasing its tail. These little moments are what make life special. Buddhism teaches us to pay attention to the small wonders around us. When you stop to admire the clouds or the way the grass tickles your toes, you're connecting with nature. It's like saying, "Thank you, world, for being so cool!" And who wouldn't want to be friends with a squirrel doing a dance?

Let's not forget that sometimes caring means helping others. Imagine you see someone struggling to carry a mountain of books. You could be their superhero by offering to help! Buddha believed that helping others is like planting seeds of kindness. They grow into beautiful flowers of friendship and joy! So, whether it's holding the door for someone or sharing your crayons, each little act counts. It's like being part of a secret club where everyone feels awesome and appreciated.

In the grand adventure of life, sharing and caring are like the magical keys that unlock happiness. They remind us that we all have a role to play, no matter how small. So next time you share your toys, help a friend, or simply smile at someone, remember that you're spreading a little bit of Buddha's wisdom. And that, my dear friends, is what makes the world a brighter, funnier, and happier place!

Daily Practices

Making Buddha Time Fun

Daily practices are like the secret sauce that makes your journey into Buddhism super tasty and fun! Imagine you're a little chef in a big kitchen, and your job is to stir up some happiness and mindfulness. The best part? You don't need a fancy hat or a long apron to get started! All you need is a sprinkle of curiosity, a dash of silliness, and a whole lot of heart.

First up on our fun-filled menu is the "Silly Breathing Game." Grab a friend, your pet goldfish, or even a stuffed animal. Sit down comfortably and pretend you're blowing up the biggest balloon ever! Take a deep breath in, hold it like you're about to pop a piñata, and then let it out with a funny sound—like a whoopee cushion! This practice not only helps you focus but also fills the room with giggles. Remember, the more ridiculous your sounds, the better your balloon gets!

Next, let's talk about "Gratitude Jars." This isn't just any jar; it's a magical jar that can hold all the good stuff that makes you smile! Grab an empty jar, some colorful paper, and crayons. Every day, write down something that made you happy—like a giant slice of pizza or a funny face your dog made. Fold it up and pop it in the jar. When you're feeling a bit down, open the jar and read your happy moments. It's like a treasure chest filled with giggles and sunshine!

Have you ever tried "Mindful Nature Walks"? This isn't just a stroll in the park; it's an adventure! As you walk, pretend you're a detective searching for the coolest things in nature. Is that a leaf shaped like a dinosaur? Or a rock that looks like a cookie? Use your senses to feel the crunch of leaves under your feet and listen for the orchestra of chirping birds. You'll be amazed at how much fun you can have while being mindful. Plus, you'll become an expert nature explorer!

Lastly, let's not forget about "Buddha Stories Time." Gather your family or friends and take turns telling funny or silly stories about the Buddha or other characters from Buddhist tales. You can even create your own quirky stories where the Buddha might ride a unicycle or have a pet monkey! This practice helps you learn about compassion and kindness while having a blast. So, get ready to laugh, share, and let your imagination run wild!

Spreading Smiles

Be the Light in Someone's Day!

Being the light in someone's day is like being a superhero without a cape! You don't need superpowers to make someone smile; all you need Is a little kind ness and a sprinkle of joy. Imagine walking into a room and seeing your friend frowning like a grumpy cat. What if you suddenly pulled a funny face or told a silly joke? The transformation is magical! That frown can turn into a giggle, and just like that, you've spread smiles like confetti at a birthday party.

Now, let's talk about small acts of kindness. They are like tiny seeds that grow into big, beautiful flowers. You can start with something simple, like sharing your favorite snack with someone who forgot their lunch. Trust me, offering a cookie can turn a bad day into a great one faster than you can say "chocolate chip"! Or how about writing a cheerful note for a class-mate who seems a bit down? A note that says, "You're awesome, and don't forget it!" can brighten their day like sunshine peeking through the clouds.

But wait, there's more! You can also be the light by being a good listener. Sometimes, people just need someone to hear them out. You could sit next to a friend and ask them how their day was. If they're feeling blue, your listening ears can be more comforting than a warm blanket on a chilly night. Plus, you might even learn some-thing new! Maybe your friend has a pet turtle named Gary, who loves to dance. Now that's a fun fact to share!

Sometimes, being the light means being a little silly. Imagine playing a game where you and your friends have to make each other laugh without using any words. You could hop around like a bunny or pretend to be a robot that can only dance sideways. Laughter is contagious, and before you know it, everyone will be rolling on the floor with giggles! Making someone laugh is one of the easiest ways to spread happiness and show them that you care.

So, remember, being the light in someone's day is about filling the world with joy, one smile at a time. Whether it's through sharing, listening, or just being a little silly, your actions can shine brightly. Next time you see a friend who needs cheering up, don't be afraid to let your inner superhero shine. Who knows? You might just make someone's day the best one ever, and that's a superpower worth celebrating!

Your Little Buddha Adventure Continues

Wow! You made it all the way to the end of Little Buddha – A Journey into Buddhism for Kids! Give yourself a big round of applause, a happy little dance, or even an extra cookie (you deserve it). But guess what? This isn't really the end. Nope, it's actually just the beginning of your own adventure into kindness, mindfulness, and all those wise little lessons we've explored together.

Throughout this book, you've met Prince Siddhartha, sat under the wise Bodhi Tree, discovered the power of a single breath, and even learned how kindness can be the greatest superpower of all. But here's the secret: these lessons aren't meant to just stay in these pages—they're meant to travel with you, wherever you go. Whether you're at school, at home, or just hanging out with your pet goldfish, you can always bring a little bit of Buddha wisdom into your day.

Maybe tomorrow you'll take a moment to sit quietly and focus on your breath, or perhaps you'll notice a friend who's feeling sad and offer them a smile or a kind word. Maybe you'll even share one of the stories from this book with someone who needs a little extra happiness in their day. Every small act of kindness, every mindful breath, and every thoughtful moment adds up to something really big—like tiny stars lighting up the night sky.

But here's the coolest part: you don't need to be perfect to keep practicing these lessons. Even the Buddha himself started as a curious kid, asking questions and searching for answers. Some days you'll feel calm and focused, like a wise old owl, and other days you might feel wiggly and distracted, like a playful monkey—and that's totally okay! What matters is that you keep showing up, keep trying, and keep being you.

Remember, Buddhism isn't about being serious all the time or sitting perfectly still. It's about finding joy in the little things, like the sound of rain tapping on your window, the taste of your favorite snack, or the feeling of the sun warming your face. It's about being present in every moment and finding gratitude in the simplest things.

So, as you close this book, take a deep breath and give yourself a little smile. You're already on your way to being a 'Little Buddha' in your own special way. And the world? Well, it's a little bit brighter now because of you.

Thank you for joining this journey. Whether it's your first step or just one of many, know that kindness, peace, and wisdom are always right there with you, ready to guide you like a warm, glowing lantern on a dark path.

Keep breathing, keep smiling, and keep being your amazing self.

The adventure continues…

Let's Meet Psalm

P salm Carnoustie is a passionate children's author dedicated to introducing young readers to the vibrant world of cultures, religions, and timeless wisdom from around the globe. With a warm and engaging storytelling style, Psalm crafts tales that spark curiosity, foster understanding, and celebrate diversity.

Believing that children are the seeds of a more compassionate future, Psalm is driven by the philosophy that early exposure to different beliefs and traditions nurtures empathy, kindness, and open-mindedness. Her books serve as gentle guides, helping children see the beauty in differences while embracing the common threads that unite us all.

When she's not weaving enchanting stories, Psalm enjoys exploring cultural festivals, collecting folklore from faraway lands, and sharing moments of quiet reflection in nature. Her stories are not just books—they are bridges, connecting little hearts to a world of understanding and acceptance.

www.ingramcontent.com/pod-product-compliance
Lightning Source LLC
LaVergne TN
LVHW051102080426
835508LV00019B/2020